THE HOME FRONT

RATIONING

Fiona Reynoldson

Wayland

THE HOME FRONT

THE BLITZ
EVACUATION
PRISONERS OF WAR
PROPAGANDA
RATIONING
WOMEN'S WAR

Editor: Mike Hirst
Series designer: Nick Cannan
Consultant: Terry Charman, researcher and historian at the Imperial War Museum

First published in 1990 by
Wayland (Publishers) Limited
61 Western Road, Hove
East Sussex BN3 1JD

British Library Cataloguing in Publication Data
Reynoldson, Fiona
Rationing.
1. Great Britain. Social conditions. Effects of World War II
I. Title II. Series
941.084

ISBN 1–85210–975–0

Typeset by Rachel Gibbs, Wayland
Printed and bound by Casterman S.A., Belgium

CONTENTS

The Need for Rationing

We risk our lives to bring you food. It's up to you not to waste it.

'A Message from our Seamen'

Above *During the First World War, there were shortages of many goods. The government put out posters such as this, encouraging people not to waste food.*

There were shortages of food in Britain during the First World War. Much of the food the British people ate came from abroad and was brought to Britain in ships. During the war, these food supplies were destroyed because many ships were sunk by German submarines. Other ships were used to bring guns to Britain instead of food.

Because food was scarce in the First World War, prices went up. Poor people could not afford enough, which was very unfair. So, towards the end of the war, the government brought in a scheme for rationing food. All the food available was then shared out more fairly.

In the late 1930s, everyone realized that, sooner or later, war would break out again in Europe. The British government decided to make preparations in many ways. New aeroplanes were designed. More ships were built. The government made plans for evacuating children from cities, and plans for dealing with bomb damage to cities and factories. The government also made plans for producing more food in Britain and for sharing it out fairly.

The government planned a new department to organize rationing. It was called the Ministry of Food.

Right *Issuing ration books. The woman in the picture is checking the books against the National Register, which contained everyone's identity card number.*

Adult's Weekly Ration in May, 1941.

3 pints milk

55 g tea

one shilling's worth meat

225 g jam

170 g butter

55 g cooking fat

225 g sugar

115 g bacon

30 g cheese

'It was set up in 1937 and headed by people from the food industry. These were people who knew about buying, selling and storing goods such as bacon, ham, butter, tea and so on. So from the first, it was a very practical ministry. Civil servants worked with and for expert grocers, bakers, butchers – the men who ran big businesses in these lines.' (Stuart Robertson, employee at the Ministry of Food, London.)

In Germany too, rationing was planned and introduced at the beginning of the war.

'Eintopf-one-pot-day this Sunday, which means all you can get for lunch is cheap stew but you pay the price of a big meal for it.' (William Shirer, *Berlin Diary*, 22 October 1939.)

Organizing Rationing

The Ministry of Food divided Britain into regions. There was a South-Eastern Region, London Region and so on.

Each region had a controller who headed a regional food office. Within the region were local food offices – usually one in each town. (There were about 1,300 local food offices in the whole of Britain.) A Food Executive Officer was in charge of the local office. He and his staff handled all the planning for rationing.

'Before rationing begins application forms would be sent to every householder, who would be asked to give particulars of everyone living in his home. These forms would be returned to the local food office which would issue the Ration Books, one for each person.' (From *Your Food In Wartime*, Public Information Leaflet No.4, July 1939.)

There were several numbers on the front of the ration book. In the middle was the identity card, or national

Below left This cartoon from 1942 shows just how vital coupons from ration books were.

Below right A ration book. Can you see the national registration (identity card) number?

"*Nothing but money, money, money! Where the blazes do they keep their coupons?*"

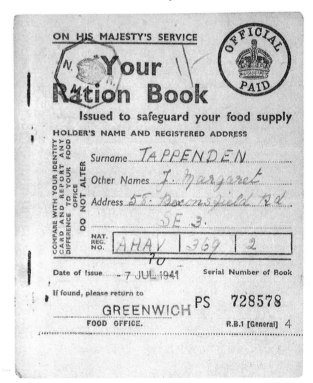

ON HIS MAJESTY'S SERVICE

OFFICIAL PAID

Your Ration Book

Issued to safeguard your food supply

HOLDER'S NAME AND REGISTERED ADDRESS

Surname TAPPENDEN

Other Names J. Margaret

Address 55 Bennsfield Rd SE 3.

NAT. REG. NO. AHAV 369 2

Date of Issue 7 JUL 1941

Serial Number of Book

If found, please return to GREENWICH FOOD OFFICE.

PS 728578

R.B.1 [General] 4

When someone went shopping, they needed coupons from ration cards as well as money.

registration, number of the owner of the ration book. (During the war everyone had to have an identity card because the government was very afraid of spies.) The book also had a serial number and stamped at the bottom was the region and local office number.

'My mother's ration books were L.86. L for London and 86 for the food office in Wimbledon.' (D. Fuller, London.)

As well as eating less like the Germans, people were asked to keep in stores of food in case of shortages.

'... the amount of stocks in any area might be affected by air-raid damage, or the flow of supplies might be reduced temporarily by transport difficulties. Food suitable for householder's storage: meat and fish in cans or glass jars; flour; suet; canned or dried milk; sugar; tea; cocoa; plain biscuits.' (From *Your Food in Wartime*.)

In the Ministry of Food, there was a Bacon and Ham Division, a Potato and Carrot Division and so on. Each division organized its own goods. For instance, cold stores were requisitioned by the Bacon and Ham Division from big butchers' businesses. All divisions worked on publicity to encourage the public to eat the kind of food that Britain could actually produce itself.

Healthy Eating

The government controlled prices so that no shops could charge high prices for food or other goods. Together with rationing, it was a way to get fair shares for all. But the Ministry of Food also wanted people to eat more healthily. This was the job of the ministry's Scientific Division.

'Pre-war surveys of the nation's diet showed that one quarter of the British population was undernourished and that half the women of the working class were in poor health, 80 per cent of under fives had some bone abnormality, 90 per cent had badly formed or decayed teeth.' (*A People's War*, Peter Lewis.)

The Scientific Division got to work.

Potato Pete and Dr Carrot encouraged people to eat home-grown vegetables.

'We knew what people needed for nutrients; we knew exactly how much nutrient and how many calories people needed for energy.' (Patty Fish, Scientific Division of the Ministry of Food.)

The Ministry of Food saw the chance to improve people's health.

'Special arrangements were made for young children and expectant and nursing mothers. There were special milk supplies, cod-liver oil and orange juice.' (Dorothy Hollingsworth, Scientific Division of the Ministry of Food.)

The Scientific Division went further. It worked out something called the 'basal diet'. If the worst came to the worst it knew exactly how little bread, potatoes, oatmeal, vegetables and milk an adult human being could survive on. Other unusual foods were suggested, such as nettle toast and dandelion fritters! However, not everyone was keen on the new foods. The prime minister, Winston Churchill, thought the basal diet sounded dreadful.

'Almost all of the food faddists I ever knew, nut-eaters and the like, have died young after a long period of senile decay . . . the way to lose the war is to try to force the British public into a diet of milk, oatmeal, potatoes, washed down on gala occasions with a little lime juice.' (Letter from Winston Churchill to Lord Woolton at the Ministry of Food.)

Below *The government tried to make sure that babies and young children had good food. In fact, many poor children were better fed during the war than they had been before it.*

'Milk of course, but don't forget Cod Liver Oil & Orange Juice'

WELFARE FOODS SERVICE

The Battle of the Atlantic

For the first few months of the war nothing much happened in Western Europe. This period between September 1939 and May 1940 was called the phoney war. To people in Britain it did not seem like a real war.

Although it might have been a phoney war on land, British ships were already being attacked by German submarines. However, in the first months there was at least plenty of meat. Farmers slaughtered many of their cows, pigs and sheep because these animals used up valuable food imported into Britain by ship.

As the war continued, more and more ships were sunk. At its worst, in 1942, one in four ships bringing food, machines, weapons, soldiers and oil to Britain was sunk. Most of these ships were sunk in the Atlantic Ocean. The ships sailed in convoys protected by destroyers and other vessels but, even so, submarines slipped in amongst them and torpedoed many.

'At the outbreak of war, Britain had 21,215,261 tons [21,554,705 tonnes] of merchant shipping afloat – more than Russia, Germany, Italy, France, Norway, Sweden and Greece put together. The vapour trails in the skies of Kent during the Battle of Britain were carved by the petrol brought in by sea; the food in the bellies of munition workers came in by sea . . .' (*The War Papers*.)

Britain depended on its ships as a lifeline. Germany realized that the Battle of the Atlantic was one of the most vital of the war for Britain.

'With enough U-boats we can and will finish off the British Isles.' (Admiral Dönitz, 1941.)

When Italy joined in the war, on the German side, half-way through 1940, the rations in Britain got even smaller as less food could come in from abroad.

'We have a certain amount of sugar saved, but of course it won't be easy after the present ration. The

People were told that they could help the war effort by saving food. Compare this poster with the one from the First World War on page four.

cut in butter will be no hardship, as nobody knows the difference (from margarine) except me.' (*Among You Taking Notes*, Naomi Mitchison.)

A convoy of twenty-four ships in the North Sea.

The Docks

When food and other goods did reach Britain in ships, the ships had to be unloaded. Then the food had to be stored. Sometimes things went wrong.

'One consignment of millions of eggs had been kept hanging about on the New York dockside and by the time it arrived, Liverpool dockers had to be paid extra to unload it. The eggs were finally disposed of by being dropped down a disused mine, by the truckload.' (*A People's War*, Peter Lewis.)

After that disaster America sent dried eggs to Britain. A large percentage of an egg is water, so dried eggs took

A Belgian ship being unloaded in London docks. However, during the Blitz ships began to sail to other, safer ports. Food and goods were then unloaded and transported to London by train. From London, they could be sent on to any part of the country.

up less space in ships. Moreover, they did not go bad. Some people hated them and said they tasted floury. But they were a good standby in cakes and other dishes.

London docks burning on the night of 7 September 1940 after a heavy German raid.

> 'I loved them in scrambled eggs and hated it after the war when we had real eggs again.' (Lesley Barnden, London.)

In the war a person was lucky if they ate one real egg every week.

Many other goods came by sea too. London was a huge port with dozens of ships plying up and down the Thames. Docks lined the river banks. Dockers unloaded the ships and put the goods in big warehouses. There were warehouses for flour, sugar, rum, tobacco, fruit, meat, wood and so on. Of course, the Germans knew how important these stores were. During the Blitz, they bombed the docks of London and many other ports as hard as they could.

> 'Sixteen warehouses holding 34 million pounds of tobacco leaf were destroyed. A little was saved for cigarettes; some was only good enough to have the nicotine extracted and the rest was treated with lime and used as much-needed fertilizer.' (*The Thames on Fire*, L.M. Bates.)

Storing and Catering

The Ministry of Food quickly realized that it must move stores away from the docks. It tried all sorts of things. At one time, flour was transferred from ships to big barges and towed up the River Thames well away from London. It stayed in the barges until it was needed by the bakeries.

The Ministry also set up buffer depots. These were simply large buildings for storing food, scattered all over the countryside. Sometimes you can see them even today, with the name 'Buffer Depot' still showing.

The ordinary housewife did not mind where the goods were stored, as long as she could feed her family. It was nearly always the women who catered for the family, often doing a war job as well; and catering in the war was almost a full-time job in itself.

The whole idea of rationing was that everyone had a fair share of what was available. So the government could not ration something unless it could guarantee it would meet the rations. Many things were not rationed

'Are you ready to cut the cake, Madam?' Although plaster wedding cakes still decorated confectioners' shop windows, real wedding cakes were a thing of the past. Icing was forbidden and there were not enough fruit, eggs or butter to make big cakes.

..*Shoot straight, Lady*

This propaganda by the Ministry of Food acknowledged that housewives played as important a part in the war effort as soldiers.

at all: they were just unobtainable. Fish, for example, was never rationed.

'Sometimes you could get fish but it was always in short supply – first come, first served. You could wait half an hour in the queue and still not get any.' (Peggy Reynoldson, Kent.)

Queuing took up a lot of time. Managing the rations needed a lot of thought and planning. For instance, dried fruit such as raisins was hardly ever seen.

'We used to go out and collect elderberries in autumn. When we dried them they were a good substitute for currants in a cake. We used haws from the hawthorn bushes, to make chutney. The autumn was a great time for gathering fruits and berries from the country. And often there were extra sugar rations so we could make jam.' (Joan Gray, Essex.)

Eating out in a British Restaurant in Liverpool. People could eat cheaply in the British Restaurants without using coupons. It was a great help to the housewife if some of the family ate some meals out.

More Vegetables

The government not only encouraged people to use wild fruits, it also encouraged them to grow more food.

There were one and a half million allotments by 1943. People grew vegetables on railway embankments, in parks, around the edges of football pitches, in window boxes and on the roofs of air-raid shelters.

'We kept chickens at the end of the garden and rabbits in a hutch. The rabbits were to eat and the fur for gloves.' (Jeff March, Yorkshire.)

Vegetable growing meant vegetable cooking. The Ministry of Food had a programme called *Kitchen Front* on the radio every morning after the eight o'clock news. Charles Hill, the radio doctor, cajoled, directed and encouraged. He recommended meatless meals and new cuts of meat.

'He wanted us to eat tripe. Nothing could persuade me that it wasn't old, white washleather, with onions or without.' (May Haverlock, Glasgow.)

In fact, even onions were quite scarce.

Keeping chickens at the end of the garden.

But potatoes and carrots never seemed to be in short supply during the war. The Ministry of Food worked hard to persuade people to eat as many of these vegetables as possible. The cartoon figures Potato Pete and Dr Carrot were invented. Carrots were full of vitamins and were said to help you to see in the dark (a great help in the blackout!). Lord Woolton, the head of the Ministry of Food invented 'Lord Woolton's Pie'. It was filled with all sorts of vegetables and topped with potatoes. Newspapers and magazines had recipes for how to make tasty dishes out of everything from potato crisps to cabbage stalks.

'. . . when the water boils add the chopped stalks. Cover with a lid and cook for four to five minutes. Add thickly sliced raw potatoes and carrots and a small piece of boiling bacon.' (*The Daily Mirror*, 30 August 1940.)

Above left *The British government urged people to grow their own vegetables with a 'Dig for Victory' campaign which lasted throughout the war.*

Above right *Even parks such as London's Hyde Park were given over to growing food.*

Farming More Land

Growing more vegetables on allotments was only one way of increasing rations. Farmers had to grow more too. In 1939 Britain imported 60 per cent of the food people ate. By 1945 Britain imported only 30 per cent of its food. Most of this change was due to improvements in farming. The Ministry of Agriculture tried to encourage farmers through posters with such slogans as:

'Plough Now! By Day and Night.'

Lights were fitted to ploughs. Men and women worked round the clock. More machines were introduced; in fact there were:

'. . . more changes probably than in the whole of the history of agriculture.' (Sir Emrys Jones, War Cultivation Officer.)

A War Agricultural Executive Committee was formed to set production targets. It graded farmers as A (very good), B (moderate) or C (needs to improve or the farm will be taken from him). The committee rationed out tractors and fertilizers. It gave advice and it provided some teams of workers to help farmers.

Above *Women could support the war effort by joining the Women's Land Army.*

Below *Planting potatoes was backbreaking work.*

Ten million acres of grassland were ploughed up to grow corn, despite a shortage of 100,000 farm workers by 1940. The shortfall was made up by the Women's Land Army and prisoners of war, a few conscientious objectors and some volunteers.

The Women's Land Army had been very successful in the First World War, so it was re-formed in 1939. It recruited 80,000 women to do essential work in farming and forestry.

During the war, more and more machines were used on British farms, often operated by women. These two women went from the north of England to work in Hertfordshire, where they would have lived in lodgings or a special hostel.

'We lifted potatoes all morning, had our lunch in a little shed and lifted potatoes all afternoon. At first my back ached like mad but I got used to it and loved the outdoor life. There were always different jobs at different times of the year.' (Jenny Sherman, Kent.)

'We had various Land Girls on this farm. One looked after my horses and we talked about poetry.' (John Stewart Collis, farmworker.)

Clothes Rationing

As the war continued, everything was in short supply. Clothes, material and footwear were rationed from 1 June 1941.

'There is enough and to spare for all if we have fair shares.' (Board of Trade Advertisement.)

The government issued everyone with a clothing coupon book. To buy clothes, people had to spend coupons as well as money. For instance, a man's shirt was five coupons, a jacket thirteen coupons and a tie one coupon. Coupons had to cover sheets and towels as well. Each person had sixty-six coupons for one year and this was later reduced to forty-eight. So everyone had to wear the same clothes for a long time.

Shorter hemlines, few buttons and very little material were used in Utility fashions. However, in the 1940s, it was still impossible to be smartly dressed without a hat.

'One simple jersey can do the work of several if you wear a necklace one day, none the next and with rolled up sleeves, the way the American girls are doing, the next.' (Ann Scott James in *Picture Post*.)

'Mend and Make Do, to Avoid Buying New,' was a slogan put out by the Board of Trade. Films were made to show that a father's old overcoat could be cut up to make a coat for a child. The cloth sacks that contained flour could be saved to make a little girl's dress.

New clothes had to be made from the least possible material. Out went wide skirts, turn-ups on men's trousers and more than four buttons on a shirt. In came Utility clothes. The Utility sign on clothes meant that they were designed (often by top designers) to use very little material and to be of a reasonable standard. Between 80 per cent and 90 per cent of the clothes on sale in shops were Utility.

'They were simple, plain and neat and we got terribly tired of them.' (Joan Sharpe, Dumbartonshire.)

As the war went on, Utility covered other things besides clothes. For instance, there was simple furniture, using the least amount of wood (often blockboard) and no trimmings.

Above left *Making do and mending was one way of stretching the clothes ration.*

Above right *Utility furniture was very plain and simple.*

The Black Market

The aim of rationing was to make sure that everyone had fair shares. But some people still managed to get hold of unofficial goods and sold them for high prices on what was called the black market. Selling goods secretly was illegal and widespread, although in Britain the black market was never huge.

'It's not clever to get more than your share.' (Ministry of Food poster.)

Most people agreed with the Ministry of Food, but, on the other hand, food shortages were never so bad in Britain that people faced hunger and starvation.

'Why should you need a black market, anyway, when you don't even have to ration bread?' (A European refugee, 1944.)

There were two types of black market. Some of the illegal food came from small, petty thefts.

Below left *Some people were more sensitive than others about any possible connection with the black market, as this cartoon shows.*

Below right *American soldiers were popular because they had goods such as chewing gum or cigarettes that were in short supply in Britain. These soldiers are distributing toys to London children at Christmas 1943.*

"Hi—what about a comma or something after my name?"

'When the fish train came in, the fish was transferred to horse-drawn wagons. Then one of the boxes would come off the back of the wagon and we'd have a couple of haddock, or four kippers on a shovel cooked up in the engine.' (An engine driver.)

Women in particular became used to queuing to buy everything from fish to clothes.

Far more serious were big thefts from warehouses, docks and factories. Ladies' stockings sold for up to five shillings a pair in markets and on street corners.

'We had a well known factory broken into one weekend. Thousands of pounds' worth of stockings were stolen, and they found their way on to the London black market.' (Jock Joiner, Leicester CID.)

Thefts from railways were very common. In 1941, about £1 million's worth of goods was stolen, but on the whole the system of rationing and fair shares worked. Although rations were even smaller after the war, Britain did not face the extreme hardship of other parts of Europe, where the black market was far bigger and more widespread.

More Shortages

In November 1941, the government introduced a points rationing system, as well as the ordinary rationing. Everyone was allowed sixteen points a month. The points ration book was pink. A person could 'spend' their points on anything they liked – the whole lot on one tin of salmon or, more thriftily, on a few tins of pilchards.

> 'Tinned fruit was such a luxury. Mum used to save the points up for a tin at Christmas time.' (Jack Peters, Glasgow.)

Biscuits, dried eggs and cereals were all available on points rationing. So was the new tinned meat from America: Spam.

If these luxuries were a pleasure, the National Wheatmeal Loaf was not. It was made of 86 per cent extraction flour (that is, using nearly all the wheat including the husks). At that time, most people still preferred white bread to brown, and the National Wheatmeal Loaf was made to look as white as possible. It finished up a dirty beige colour.

An advertisement for Spam in 1944. Tinned meat was relatively easy to bring over from the USA in ships.

> 'So will I bow to dear brown bread,
> Because, as my wise rulers say,
> We shall save tonnage in this way.
> But let this point be understood –
> No man can tell me it is good.'
> (A.P. Herbert, writer.)

At least bread was never rationed or unobtainable in Britain during the war. However, foreign fruits, such as oranges, were rarely seen.

> 'They've got some oranges in the village but they'll only sell them to children and they have to bring a note from the clinic to say they need them.' (From the Mass-Observation Archive.)

The more ships that were sunk in the Atlantic Ocean, the more rations were reduced and some goods became completely unobtainable. By 1942 the war was biting hard. Paper was in short supply. Envelopes were used over and over again. Glass was scarce. At one time you could only buy a bottle of beer if you took back an empty bottle at the same time. Petrol was also very scarce, and after 1942 people were not allowed to use petrol for private cars at all. It was even difficult to find new, replacement valves for radio sets.

Above *People were urged not to leave the radio switched on unless they were really listening – it wasted valves.*

Left *These boys in Lancashire spent their spare time collecting waste paper, bottles, tins and silver paper in 1940. In many streets there were pig bins, where people could put scraps of food to feed local pigs. Bones (for glue) and aluminium (used in aeroplanes) were also collected.*

The German Home Front

Germany had started rationing in 1939. Each family had seven food cards. The blue one was for meat, the green for eggs and so on. Extra rations went to workers in heavy industry, expectant and nursing mothers, blood and human milk donors, sick people and vegetarians. Because of the Nazi Party's attitude to the Jews, Jewish people had lower rations.

As in Britain, rations were fixed for four weeks at a time. For one week in 1939, rations were: 1 lb (453g) of meat; 5 lbs (2.2kg) of bread; 12 oz (340g) fats; 12 oz (340g) sugar; 1 lb (453g) ersatz coffee, made of roasted barley seeds and acorns.

It was estimated that 40 per cent of Germans ate better than ever before, but:

'The only item that is adequate is bread, the weekly ration of 5 lbs [2.2 kg] for average consumers and 7½ lbs [3.4 kg] for day workers being more than even a German labourer is accustomed to eating.' (*The German Home Front*, Terry Charman.)

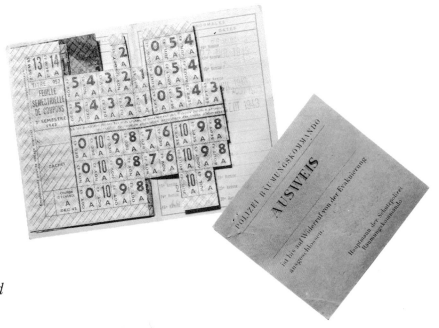

Ration and identity cards issued in German-occupied France.

Left *By the end of the war many people in central and eastern Europe were desperately short of food. This picture shows someone digging in the rubble of a bombed-out house for potatoes. People were also known to cut up dead horses lying by the side of the road for meat.*

Below *When he came to power, Hitler promised Germans that they would be able to buy their own Volkswagen cars if they saved one mark a week. In fact, because of shortages and rationing, German people could not buy Volkswagens until long after the war.*

By the autumn of 1939, petrol rationing was stringent and clothes rationing was introduced on a points system (which the British copied). Shoes were in very short supply. You could only have two pairs and had to show that one was worn out in order to replace them. Soap was scarce too.

'The odour of stale sweat from bodies that work hard and have only a cube of soap as big as a penny box of matches to wash with for a month, lingers in the subway trains.' (Howard K. Smith, reporter, 1941.)

Whenever Germany conquered a new country, goods flooded in. For instance, there were silk stockings by the trainload when Germany conquered France. But by the last years of the war, trains to Berlin brought only wounded soldiers from the eastern front.

5 Mark die Woche musst Du sparen willst Du im eignen Wagen fahren

World Shortages

After 1942, conditions in Germany and the rest of mainland Europe deteriorated. The war made it difficult for ships to move freely. Moreover, the fighting disrupted food production.

'Food production per head declined by about 12 per cent, a much heavier decrease in Continental Europe and the Far East being only partially offset by increase (in food production) in North America and the British Isles.' (*Food, Famine and Relief*, published by the League of Nations, 1946.)

In America and the British Commonwealth, rationing was mostly limited to animal foodstuffs. There was little real restriction. Britain, Ireland, Denmark, Sweden and Switzerland on the whole maintained a reasonable level of food. In Germany and the USSR, food intake was

Below left The cathedral rising above the rubble in Cologne. Many German cities were heavily bombed by the Allies.

Below right German food officers questioning a farmer's wife in 1947. After the war, many farmers did not want to sell their food for money, but preferred to barter for goods such as coffee, machines, shoes and cigarettes.

Under the Marshall Aid plan, enormous amounts of food and money were sent to Europe from America after the war.

slightly lower; it was lower still in Belgium, Finland, the Netherlands and Norway; lower again in France and Italy, and even more so in Poland, Greece and Yugoslavia. Parts of India and China saw actual famine in 1943, and Japan suffered badly at the end of the war. There was rationing in many of these areas, though often, as in Africa, rationing was hard to organize and meant just giving out sacks of food for village leaders to distribute. In every country, city dwellers seemed to suffer from food shortages more than the people who lived in the country.

The war ended in 1945, but the shortages became worse. Cities, railways, ships and large areas of farmland had been destroyed.

'. . . hunger hangs over the homes of more than 800,000,000 people.' (Herbert Hoover, president of the USA, 1946.)

International food relief began in April 1945 but it would take years for Europe, the USSR and the Far East to recover.

'Houses without doors, roofs, windows,
The rain will wash us all away,
Men as thin and pale as ghosts,
Rations smaller every day.'
(German popular rhyme of the time.)

GLOSSARY

Abnormality   Something which is not normal.

Allotments   Small pieces of land, where people grow vegetables and fruit in their spare time.

Basal diet   A diet worked out during the war. It was the minimum amount of food needed to keep someone healthy.

Black market   Buying and selling goods illegally.

Blitz   The bombing of London and other British cities by the German air force.

Blockboard   Two thin sheets of wood, with a sandwich filling of other, softer woods.

Conscientious objectors   People who refuse to go into the army because they disagree with fighting.

Consignment   A delivery of goods.

Donors   People who give something.

Ersatz   Substitute.

Gala occasions   Special holidays.

Imported   Brought into the country from abroad.

Merchant shipping   Ships which carry goods, such as food or oil.

Nazi Party   The political party that ruled Germany from 1933–45 and was led by Adolf Hitler.

Nicotine   The drug inside cigarettes.

Nutrients   The substances in food that give you energy and make you healthy.

Phoney war   The period in late 1939 and early 1940, when there was no fighting in western Europe.

Requisitioned   Taken over by the government.

Senile decay   Loss of memory and thinking power in old age.

Thriftily   Being careful not to waste anything.

Tonnage   The amount of goods that a ship can carry.

Tripe   White-coloured meat from the lining of a cow's stomach.

U-boat   A submarine used by the German navy.

Undernourished   Without enough food to eat.

PROJECTS

1 Weigh out and write down the weight of food you eat in a week. Compare the amount of food you eat with the amount of rationed food you would have eaten in the Second World War. Remember you have to include whatever fats, butter and so on you eat in cakes, biscuits, pastry, etc. A direct comparison will be difficult because you are eating a much more varied diet than you would have done in wartime.

You could also try living on wartime rations for a week! But remember, if you eat out you do not have to count that food in your rations.

2 Ask neighbours, friends and relations for recipes they used or made up during the war. You can make your own recipe book and then try some of them out.

BOOKS TO READ

Books for older readers

Susan Briggs, *Keep Smiling Through* (Fontana, 1976)
E.R. Chamberlin, *Life in Wartime Britain* (Batsford, 1972)
Terry Charman, *The German Home Front* (Barrie & Jenkins, 1989)
Peter Lewis, *A People's War* (Methuen/Thames, 1986)
Norman Longmate, *How We Lived Then* (Hutchinson, 1971)

Books for younger readers

Richard Gibbs, *Children at War* (Mass-Observation Archive, University of Sussex Library, 1987)
Fiona Reynoldson, *War at Home* (Heinemann Educational Books, 1980)
Stewart Ross, *How They Lived – A Family in World War II* (Wayland, 1985)

INDEX

Numbers in **bold** refer to illustrations

ACKNOWLEDGEMENTS

The publishers would like to thank the following for permitting us to quote from their sources. (The order of sources is as they appear in the text.) Barrie & Jenkins Ltd. for *The German Home Front 1939–45* by Terry Charman, 1989. Thames and Hudson Ltd. for *A People's War* by Peter Lewis, 1986. Victor Gollancz Ltd. for *Among You Taking Notes: The Wartime Diary 1939–45* by Naomi Mitchison, 1985. Marshall Cavendish Partworks for *The War Papers*, 1976. Terence Dalton Ltd. for *The Thames on Fire* by L.M. Bates, 1985. Extracts from Mass-Observation copyright the Trustees of the Tom Harrisson Mass-Observation Archive, reproduced by permission of Curtis Brown Group Ltd. Barrie & Jenkins Ltd. for *The Worm Forgives the Plough, A Diary of a Farmworker* by John Stewart Collis, 1988. Where sources have a name and location only, they were interviewed by the author.

The illustrations in this book were supplied by the following: ET Archive 8, 26; Mary Evans Picture Library 6(right); Hulton Picture Library 4(below), 7, 9(above), 11, 12, 21(right), 22(right), 25(left), 27(above), 28(both); Imperial War Museum 4(above), 10, 17(right), 21(left); Peter Newark 6(left), 15(above), 17(left), 18(above), 24, 25(right); Popperfoto 19; Punch 14, 22(left); Topham Picture Library 9(below), 13, 15(below), 16, 18(below), 20, 23, 29; Weimar Archive 27(below). The artwork is by John Yates.